ORDINARY
PEOPLE
CHANGE
— THE —
WORLD

I am
Ruth Bader Ginsburg

BRAD MELTZER

illustrated by Christopher Eliopoulos

 ROCKY POND BOOKS

I am **RUTH BADER GINSBURG.**

How do you create change?

I was born with the name Joan Ruth Bader, but my sister changed it to the nickname Kiki since I was such a kicky baby.

In kindergarten, my name got changed again. There were so many girls named Joan that my family started calling me Ruth.

One of the hardest things to change is what the world thinks of you. Growing up in Brooklyn, New York, I liked the things most kids liked: roller-skating, riding bikes, and playing games like stoop-ball.

When I was little, people expected different things from boys and girls. In some of the earliest books I read, boys would be climbing trees and riding bikes, while girls would just sit around in pink dresses.

Thankfully, my parents didn't accept the way things were.

My father was an immigrant whose only formal schooling was at night, to learn English.

My mother got a job and never had a chance to attend college. Only her brother did. Since he was a boy, the family thought his education was more important.

My parents wanted a better life for me, and they knew how to get it.

Every week, my mother took me on our Friday afternoon adventure to the library.

I'd pick out five books, like *Little Women* and *The Secret Garden*.

OOH, THIS FEISTY ONE JO IS MY FAVORITE.

I also enjoyed Greek mythology.

And I loved doing what you're doing right now: reading about *real* female heroes.

AMELIA EARHART

HARRIET TUBMAN

Since we were Jewish, my mother also introduced me to Jewish women of valor—the boldest and bravest of them all.

EMMA LAZARUS

HENRIETTA SZOLD

LILLIAN WALD

These women stood for the Jewish idea of "tikkun olam"—repairing the world—which means helping make the world a better place.

To teach me the value of helping others, on my birthday my mother would take me to the local Jewish orphanage, where we'd give away ice cream to everyone.

Sure, it would've been nice to have my own party, but I knew how much it mattered to those who had so little.

Being Jewish, I also learned that there were people who didn't like me just because of my religion.

Hatred is similar to injustice—both are destructive fractures in our society that we must repair.

Today, people know me for my intelligence.
But I wasn't great in every subject.
In eighth grade, boys had to take woodshop, while girls were forced to take classes in sewing and cooking.

Mine was a mess.

THIS IS UNFAIR.

I'D RATHER TAKE WOODSHOP THAN SEW.

JUST DO WHAT YOU'RE SUPPOSED TO DO.

The assignment was to sew our own graduation gowns.

Thankfully, my mother had it fixed by a local dressmaker.

When I was seventeen, my mother died.
She was the strongest and bravest person I knew.
She changed my world and taught me one of life's great lessons:
There's nothing a woman can't accomplish.

At Cornell University, a professor helped me understand that one of the great ways to change unfair things is through our legal system.

Understanding the law is like understanding the rules.

The problem was, back then, people didn't think women should go to law school.

And they certainly didn't think *Jewish* women should.

I never let that stop me.

I went to Harvard Law School and then Columbia Law School. When I started, there were nine women and five hundred men. There wasn't even a women's bathroom in the main building!

I was selected for the law review—an honor for top students—at both schools, the first woman to do so.

Did I mention that I achieved this while becoming a mother and taking care of my husband while he had cancer?

At my law school graduation, I was tied for first place in my class. But because I was a woman, there wasn't a single law firm in New York City that would hire me.

Luckily, one of my law professors convinced a local judge to take a chance.

Sometimes the only way to make change is when someone gives you a chance.

From there, I studied the law in other countries and became a law professor.

While in Sweden, I discovered that they had lots of women enrolled in law school.

I even saw a judge who was pregnant.

Other times, you won't know change is possible until someone *shows* you it's possible.

When I started teaching at Rutgers Law School, my female students helped spark my interest in a developing field of law.

A NEARBY SCHOOL HAS A CLASS ON WOMEN AND LAW.

WHAT DO YOU THINK ABOUT TEACHING THAT HERE?

I THINK THAT'S A FINE IDEA.

To prepare, I read every federal decision ever published about women's rights.

It didn't take long. There weren't many.

WOMEN ARE NOT BEING TREATED AS EQUAL CITIZENS.

Eventually, I put that knowledge to work for the American Civil Liberties Union.

Back then, even our local college was boys only.

THAT'S NOT FAIR.

GIRLS SHOULD HAVE THE SAME ACCESS TO EDUCATION AS BOYS.

We helped change the admission policy so girls could study there too.

My coworkers and I saw how many unfair laws existed.

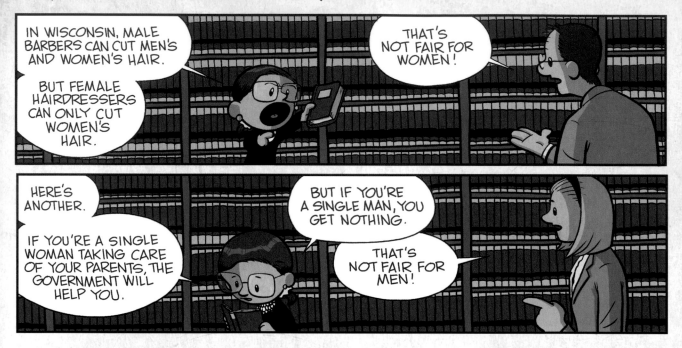

IN WISCONSIN, MALE BARBERS CAN CUT MEN'S AND WOMEN'S HAIR.

BUT FEMALE HAIRDRESSERS CAN ONLY CUT WOMEN'S HAIR.

THAT'S NOT FAIR FOR WOMEN!

HERE'S ANOTHER.

IF YOU'RE A SINGLE WOMAN TAKING CARE OF YOUR PARENTS, THE GOVERNMENT WILL HELP YOU.

BUT IF YOU'RE A SINGLE MAN, YOU GET NOTHING.

THAT'S NOT FAIR FOR MEN!

We took them to court to strike down these laws.

WE AGREE WITH YOU, MRS. GINSBURG.

IT *IS* UNFAIR TO HELP WOMEN BUT NOT MEN.

WE WON!

MORITZ VS. COMMISSIONER (1972)

Oftentimes, change doesn't happen all at once.
It happens little by little, case by case.

All we wanted was for women and men to have the same rights.
To achieve that, we needed to change more than the laws.
We had to change how people think.
It came down to a simple question:

HOW WOULD YOU LIKE THE WORLD TO BE FOR **YOUR** DAUGHTERS AND GRANDDAUGHTERS?

One of my biggest cases was about a woman named Sally Reed and a law in Idaho that said when you're choosing someone for a certain job, you should always choose a man before you choose a woman.

I co-wrote the brief that we sent to the Supreme Court, which is the most powerful court in the country.

I found out the result on a train.

REED V. REED (1971)

We won unanimously, which means every member of the Supreme Court voted for our side.

It was the first time in history that the Court struck down a law like that for being unfair to women.

Soon, I got to argue my first case at the Supreme Court.

It looked just like the temples from my old mythology books.

I wore my mother's jewelry to honor her.

Nine Justices (which is what they call the judges)— all of them men—stared down at me.

I was definitely nervous.

But once I started speaking, the Justices got to hear what life was like...

FRONTIERO V. RICHARDSON (1973)

when people treat you like a second-class citizen.

WEINBERGER V. WEISENFELD (1975)

At the podium, I had to lower the microphone.

=AHEM=

In each case, our argument was the same.

LAWS THAT STEREOTYPE ABOUT "THE WAY WOMEN AND MEN ARE" ARE OFTEN UNFAIR TO BOTH.

DUREN V. MISSOURI (1979)

Over the years, we won five out of the six Supreme Court cases I argued.

In the process, we changed the way people are treated.

Eventually, I wasn't just arguing in front of the court.
I became a judge, and then a Supreme Court Justice,
the second woman and first Jewish woman ever.

I HAVE A LAST THANK-YOU. IT IS TO MY MOTHER.

I PRAY THAT I MAY BE ALL THAT SHE WOULD HAVE BEEN HAD SHE LIVED IN AN AGE WHEN WOMEN COULD ASPIRE AND ACHIEVE.

These were the same arguments I'd heard for decades.
This time, though, I would be one of the people voting.

Every Justice but one
agreed with me that the
school treated women
unfairly and had to
change their policies.

More important, at other public schools, they can't do that to girls either.

During my time on the Supreme Court, I wasn't always on the winning side. In fact, I lost a lot.

In one case, a woman named Lilly Ledbetter was being paid less than her male coworkers for doing the same job.

My dissent told Congress that my fellow Justices misunderstood the existing law.

Within two years, Congress listened and created a new law.

In my life, they told me that women couldn't climb trees,
couldn't have adventures,
couldn't be lawyers,
and certainly couldn't be a Supreme Court Justice.
But there's *nothing* that a woman cannot be.

I was as smart and capable as anyone else—but because I was a woman, I wasn't given the same opportunities.

So how do you change things when the rules are unfair?

At some point, there will be things you want to change.
People might call you a complainer or troublemaker.
They'll tell you that things are fine the way they are.
But when you see something that's unjust, you need to take a stand.
Use your voice. Use your brain.
If people ignore you, let them hear your dissent.
You may not win now, but you can open
minds tomorrow.

ROCHELLE SHORETZ

PHIL WEISER

LAURA BRILL

JANE GINSBURG

JAMES GINSBURG

EQUAL JUS

Today, they call me a trailblazer.
But the best part of blazing a trail is leaving tracks.
That means you're not just doing things for yourself.
You're leaving a path for others to follow.
Start with one voice and let it grow into a chorus.

I am Ruth Bader Ginsburg.
Create equality, create justice.

NDER LAW ·

SONIA
SOTOMAYOR

AMY
CONEY BARRETT

ELENA
KAGAN

KETANJI
BROWN JACKSON

SANDRA
DAY O'CONNOR

"Fight for the things that you care about, but do it in a way that will lead others to join you."
—RUTH BADER GINSBURG

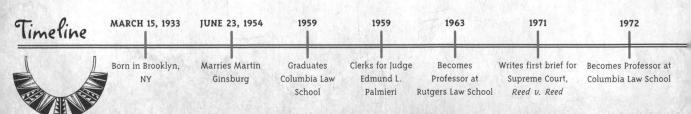

Timeline

MARCH 15, 1933	JUNE 23, 1954	1959	1959	1963	1971	1972
Born in Brooklyn, NY	Marries Martin Ginsburg	Graduates Columbia Law School	Clerks for Judge Edmund L. Palmieri	Becomes Professor at Rutgers Law School	Writes first brief for Supreme Court, *Reed v. Reed*	Becomes Professor at Columbia Law School

Ruth in 1977

Ruth being sworn in as
Supreme Court Justice

All the justices in
Ruth's first year

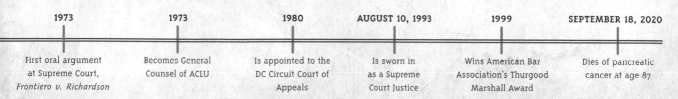

1973	1973	1980	AUGUST 10, 1993	1999	SEPTEMBER 18, 2020
First oral argument at Supreme Court, *Frontiero v. Richardson*	Becomes General Counsel of ACLU	Is appointed to the DC Circuit Court of Appeals	Is sworn in as a Supreme Court Justice	Wins American Bar Association's Thurgood Marshall Award	Dies of pancreatic cancer at age 87

In memory of Rochelle Shoretz,
dear friend and founder of Sharsheret,
who changed the rules and the laws,
forever leaving tracks to benefit others

And in memory of Justice Ruth Bader Ginsburg,
who always showed me kindness
—B.M.

For Jodi Reamer,
a sharp legal mind,
a quick wit, and
a great judge of talent
—C.E.

For historical accuracy, we used Ruth Bader Ginsburg's actual words whenever possible. For more of her true voice, we recommend and acknowledge the below works. Special thanks to Professor Jane Ginsburg, as well as Mary Hartnett and Debbie Levy for their input on early drafts.

. . . .

SOURCES

My Own Words by Ruth Bader Ginsburg with Mary Hartnett and Wendy W. Williams (Simon & Schuster, 2018)

Ruth Bader Ginsburg: The Last Interview and Other Conversations (Melville House, 2020)

Conversations with RBG: Ruth Bader Ginsburg on Life, Love, Liberty, and Law edited by Jeffrey Rosen (Holt, 2019)

Ruth Bader Ginsburg: A Life by Jane Sherron De Hart (Vintage, 2020)

The Notorious RBG: The Life and Times of Ruth Bader Ginsburg by Irin Carmon and Shana Knizhnik (Harper Collins, 2015)

RBG movie directed by Betsy West and Julie Cohen (2018)

FURTHER READING FOR KIDS

Who Was Ruth Bader Ginsburg? by Patricia Brennan Demuth (Penguin Workshop, 2019)

What Is the Supreme Court? by Jill Abramson (Penguin Workshop, 2022)

I am Sonia Sotomayor by Brad Meltzer (Rocky Pond, 2018)

I Dissent by Debbie Levy and Elizabeth Baddeley (Simon & Schuster, 2016)

. . . .

ROCKY POND BOOKS
An imprint of Penguin Random House LLC, New York

First published in the United States of America by Rocky Pond Books, an imprint of Penguin Random House LLC, 2024

Text copyright © 2024 by Forty-four Steps, Inc.
Illustrations copyright © 2024 by Christopher Eliopoulos • Coloring by K.J. Díaz with Christopher Eliopoulos

Visit us online at PenguinRandomHouse.com.

Library of Congress Cataloging-in-Publication Data is available.

Photo on page 38 (2006) by Mark Wilson/Getty Images. Photo of the 1993 Supreme Court Justices on page 39 by Diana Walker/Getty Images. Photo of Ruth in 1977 courtesy of Bettmann.
Photo of Ruth being sworn in as a Supreme Court justice by Mark Reinstein/Corbis via Getty Images.

Printed in the United States of America • ISBN 9780593533338 • 10 9 8 7 6 5 4 3

TOPL

Design by Jason Henry • Text set in Triplex • The artwork for this book was created digitally.